# The Other Me

## Poetic Thoughts on ADD
## For Adults, Kids and Parents

## Wilma R. Fellman, M.Ed., LPC

Illustrated by Arnold C. Fellman, M.D.

Foreword by Arthur L. Robin, Ph.D.

Specialty Press, Inc.
Plantation, Florida

Specialty Press, Inc.
300 Northwest 70th Avenue, Suite 102
Plantation, Florida 33317
(954) 792-8100 • (800) 233-9273


**Library of Congress Cataloging-in-Publication Data**

Fellman, Wilma R., 1946-
    The other me: poetic thoughts on ADD for adults, kids and parents /
Wilma R. Fellman
        p.    cm.
    ISBN 1-886941-16-5
    1. Attention-deficit-disorder children--Poetry. 2. Attention
-deficit disorder in adult--Poetry.    I. Title.
PS3556.E47253074        1997
811' .54--dc21                                            97-7215
                                                            CIP

*I dedicate this book to my son Jeff who has taken the difficult journey with me from confusion and frustration to knowledge and understanding. I will be forever grateful for his tenacious spirit that allowed us to grow together. With great pride and love I have come to appreciate what he has taught me about ADD: the beauty and strength of differences.*

# The Other Me
## Poetic Thoughts on ADD

## Contents

### Introduction

### For Adults & Kids

## For Parents

## Introducing Charlotte Booth

****

# Acknowledgments

I wish to acknowledge and thank several people for their contribution to this book. A few years ago, I approached my artistic husband, asking him to draw a hybrid animal that would represent how I see myself. A squirrtle would portray an animal with only two speeds: lively and squirrel-like, and then turtle-like, totally pulling in to re-group energies. Arnie created the adorable squirrtle that we see throughout this book. I feel especially lucky to have shared this rewarding project with my life partner, who has devoted countless hours to each unique illustration. I thank Arnie for all of the time cheerfully spent after his day job...his medical practice. He represents someone with "many sides of self." I also thank him endlessly for understanding the strengths and shortcomings of the squirrtle, and choosing to build our life around them.

I want to thank my sons, Rick Danuloff and Jeff Danuloff, for putting up with an "ADD mother" who often lost track of permission slips, puzzle pieces, and trains of thought. They taught me the power of humor as a survival tool. I am extremely proud of both of these young men, who each possess more strengths than I ever dreamed possible. I thank my lovely "daughter," Lainie Fellman Geary, and son-in-law, Peter Geary, for their encouraging words that I've come to love and respect. Their constant "sparkle" is a source of uplifting inspiration.

My mother, Betty Zaft, is responsible for making me feel that I was a very special and unique individual. My father, Henry Zaft, gave me an extraordinary gift...an example of  human dignity not to be compromised, and a passion for expressive writing.

I am exceedingly grateful to my publisher at Specialty Press, Inc., Dr. Harvey C. Parker, for his enthusiasm in this project, his gentle direction, and for his willingness to take on an off-the-beaten-track book. I appreciate the input of Sandra Redemske of Redemske Design and Carmine Cillo of Countywide Printing for their technical assistance.

Blessed with a warm family and supportive friends, I thank my two sisters: Arline Bittker, who taught me to stay on track with The Two H's: Humor and Hugs; and Madelon Yarows, who has shown me the positive rewards of working at close relationships regardless of distance; my wonderful parents-in-law, Dr. Abe and Betty Fellman, who proudly speak of my accomplishments on their side of the world in San Diego; my two sisters-in-law, Alice Ehrinpreis and Debbie Fellman, for their daily editing and pep talks via the miracles of E-Mail; and my "almost sister," Janice Cohen, who constantly supports and critiques with honesty, love and kindness.

I acknowledge a former counseling supervisor and continuous friend, Rosemary Doyle, for sharing her optimistic philosophy, that we grow most when we take risks and step off the comfort zone. Sharing my pain with the world as I have in this book is a prime example of stepping off my comfort zone. As counselors, we advocate that our clients do this, and I proudly dare to take my own advice.

The ADD community has led me to some wonderful colleagues and friends. I want to thank Dr. Jennifer Bramer for serving as a devoted mentor, answering dozens of questions about the publishing process as well as the apprehensions of public acceptance. I am indeed grateful for the support and encouragement of Sari Solden, MS, MFCC, and Dr. Arthur Robin who have also become trusted friends, willing to listen and advise. Their guidance has been invaluable. I am especially overwhelmed with the generous words written in Dr. Robin's foreword.

I appreciate the willingness of young Charlotte Booth to share powerful, private feelings in her poetic contribution. I'm delighted to be able to give her an opportunity to be heard.

Finally, I thank my many clients who have shared their struggles with me. Their viewpoints have allowed me to consider how deeply ADD affects fellow squirrtles. From all of them I continue to understand, learn, and accept. Together we will continue to grow.

Wilma R. Fellman
April, 1997

# Foreword
## by Arthur L. Robin, Ph.D.

Whether or not the individual with ADD will really "rest in peace" or have "eternal spin" in heaven may be a matter only God can know, but there's no debating the fact that ADD individuals now truly have poetic justice here on earth. Wilma Fellman has elevated the ADD experience to a new height of poetic justice, giving the non-ADD world a unique perspective on this disorder. If you have ADD, you will resonate to these poems, and feel validated as well as uplifted. If you don't have ADD, you will come to understand the world of Attention Deficit Disorder as you never have before, through the eyes, ears, words, images, metaphors and iambic pentameters of Wilma Fellman.

Wilma is an adult with ADD, a parent of a child with ADD, a vocational counselor who helps adolescents and adults with ADD, and above all, a poet with ADD. Through her four-fold associations with ADD, she has come to understand and express eloquently the inner workings of the mind of the person with this disorder. Her poems chronicle the experiences of the ADD individual across the lifespan, from childhood through adulthood, and even into the afterlife.

I will give a few of my favorite examples. In *Lima Beans, Broccoli and Liver,* she tells us of the agony, anxiety, and pain of the 11 year old who can't keep up in school and can't come up with the right answer when called upon by the teacher. The mental restlessness and distraction of the upbeat ADD adult who is looking towards a brighter future comes through in *I'm Destined for Greatness,* while a number of other poems bemoan the terribly frustrating side of being mentally restless, distractible, and forgetful, e.g. *Black Hole,* and *Block It Out.* The reader will come to understand the guilt and anxiety about passing for "normal" through poems such as *Backstage,* and *Dread.* The woes of an ADD parent colliding with an ADD child come through loud and clear in *5,4,3,2,1...* and the agony of the daily battle of will between parent and ADD child are apparent in *Fingers In A Long Bath.* I must admit, though, that my absolute favorite poem is *May I Rest In Peace.* The images of a messy cloud, wings that need dry cleaning, and "eternal spin," along with the thought of "faking" in heaven are precious.

In addition to Wilma's poems, she also included a moving piece, *Trapped,* by Charlotte Booth, a young adolescent with ADD. As if all this were not enough, we also have Mr. Squirrtle's masterful illustrations to give wings to Wilma's vision and carry them over hill and dale. These wings need no dry cleaning. They complement the text nicely and add a playful vision to a songful text.

We have books, videos, and songs about ADD, but until now we have not had an entire book of poetry. There is not a better person than Wilma Fellman to correct this deficiency, which she has done with style, humor, empathy, and a great deal of insight.

Arthur L. Robin, Ph.D.
Professor of Psychiatry and Behavioral Neurosciences
Wayne State University School of Medicine
Detroit, Michigan

# INTRODUCTION

# A Note to the Reader

Over fifteen years ago, I became painfully aware of the cruel ramifications of an Attention Deficit Disorder (ADD). In those years, we knew relatively little about the causes, manifestations, and emotional toll of ADD. This was long before it was "fashionable" to be interested in ADD/ADHD, and the number of knowledgeable experts was limited.

As our family struggled to cope with the erratic, tension-producing nature of ADD, I learned how deeply rooted it was in our physiology. I realized that I had always lived inside an ADD body and, as with many adults, painful childhood memories began to make sense. I built my career counseling practice with special interest for those individuals experiencing similar challenges. It is with this vantage point that I approached writing this book.

Thankfully, we now have an abundance of materials related to all aspects of ADD. We are fortunate to have so many qualified professionals sharing their expertise in ways that enlighten, clarify, and assist individuals in becoming more comfortable with their challenges...more aware of their strengths.

What I hope I have added with this book is a sensitive, lighter look at ADD from within the chaotic workings of the head and heart. While I do know firsthand how it feels to have ADD, I also believe strongly that it results in as many strengths as it does challenges.

When we can learn to laugh at ourselves, hug each other during painful times, and touch each other from the heart every chance we get...then we are truly evolving.

# About Attention Deficit Disorders

I find it ironic that I spent over half of my life hiding the symptoms of ADD, and will now seek to convince people that it does exist, and that I am, in fact, a member of this community. In order to describe ADD properly, I want to start with some of the comments I receive that demonstrate a lack of knowledge about this disorder:

- You can't have ADD because you have a Master's Degree.
- You can't have ADD because you are organized.
- You can't have ADD because you are bright.
- You can't have ADD because you aren't "hyper."
- You can't have ADD because it wasn't obvious to others in your childhood.
- You can't have ADD because you are jumping on a popular bandwagon, attributing any normal frustrations to this "new" diagnosis.
- Lazy people use ADD as an excuse.
- Everybody has ADD symptoms sometimes, so why a diagnosis?
- [And my all time favorite] Since there are too many people diagnosed with ADD today, it can't possibly exist.

ADD is presumed to be a neurological disorder that affects the central nervous system. According to the *Diagnostic Manual of Mental Disorders: Fourth Edition (DSM IV)*, published by the American Psychiatric Association, there are three subtypes of Attention-Deficit/Hyperactivity Disorder:

1. Combined Type (both inattentive and hyperactive-impulsive)
2. Predominantly Inattentive Type
3. Predominantly Hyperactive-Impulsive Type

While all individuals with ADD experience the disorder differently, common symptoms include:

Inattentive Type
- Difficulty paying attention to details
- Difficulty sustaining attention
- Trouble listening when spoken to
- Difficulty following through on instructions or with tasks
- Difficulty organizing tasks and activities
- Avoiding tasks which require sustained concentration
- Losing things often
- Being easily distracted
- Being forgetful

Hyperactive-Impulsive Type
- Fidgetiness
- Trouble sitting for long periods
- Frequently feeling restless
- Difficulty in quietly engaging in leisure activities
- Often "on the go"
- Talking excessively
- Blurting out
- Difficulty waiting his/her turn
- Interrupting often

For purposes of simplicity, I will refer to all types of the disorder by the generic term, "ADD."

Typically six or more symptoms in one of the two categories must be present for the diagnosis of ADD to be considered. In addition, five other requirements are needed:

1. Symptoms must be more frequent and severe than in others of similar age.
2. Symptoms must have been present before the age of seven.
3. Symptoms must be observed in more than one primary setting.
4. Symptoms must interfere with social, academic, or occupational functioning.
5. Symptoms are not the result of another disorder.

Current research indicates that difficulties in brain functioning in the frontal lobe may be responsible, in part, for symptoms of ADD. This area of the brain is involved in regulation of behavior, inhibition of impulses, sequential thinking, and planning and organizing. These higher order cognitive processes are sometimes referred to as Executive Function.

Furthermore, researchers suspect that malfunctions in the way certain neurotransmitter chemicals operate within the frontal lobe of the brain (and elsewhere) may be responsible for some of the problems experienced by those with ADD. Dopamine, norepinephrine, serotonin, and other neurotransmitters may be involved. Medications used to treat ADD are thought to have an effect on the supply of these neurotransmitters for use by the brain and can be very helpful in the treatment of ADD.

Therefore, it is important to remember that for a diagnosis of ADD, we need to look carefully at the following:

A. Does the individual meet the criteria for ADD now?
B. Did the individual meet the diagnostic criteria in the past?
C. Have all of the possible ADD look-alikes been ruled out?

## Fellman's User-Friendly Explanation

I like to think of ADD as a "wiring problem." For the reasons stated above, those of us with ADD are wired just a little differently, causing us to operate much like a lamp with faulty wiring: sometimes our connections allow us to burn continuously bright (maybe even brighter than the average person); sometimes our connections "flicker" when our brain function is "out of kilter;" and sometimes our connections are very off. Now, the tricky part is that we have no warning about which way we will be wired each day. This leads to inconsistency and frustration. Most individuals with ADD mask the flickering moments well, and tend to retreat when the connections are off. Therefore, those around us often observe a high functioning individual and thereby discount that there is a problem.

I understand the doubts and fears of skeptics who say that this is totally blown out of proportion; "everybody experiences these symptoms sometimes, so what's the big deal?" I can only answer by saying that everybody gets depressed sometimes too...but not all of these people would be diagnosed with a clinical depression. ADD works much the same way. Everybody does experience some of these symptoms some of the time. For an ADD diagnosis, it is a matter of frequency and severity of symptoms and degree of interference with the individual's endeavors.

ADD is not to be used as an excuse. I believe it is essential for individuals to understand how the disorder manifests in them, in order to modify their lives to "get the job done" just as well as those without the disorder.

ADD exists. It often feels horrible to live inside a "lamp with faulty wiring." Individuals with ADD can be bright, accomplished, creative beings who also have the challenges of a neurological system that betrays them now and then. Medications and/or coping strategies are now available for anyone who seeks help. Bookstores and libraries are filled with related materials. Professionals are available to help share their expertise. No one needs to feel shame anymore. No one needs to feel like a *fake*. The ADD population can now learn, grow, accept, modify, enhance and be admired for all the strength of "fellow Squirrtles." It has taken me a long time to let the world in on *The Other Me*. I do hope these poems touch similar souls and help them gain acceptance and peace.

# For Adults & Kids

**A Squirrtle?**

So tell me what you think you are
Which animal describes you?
Our class assignment wasn't hard
It's something that we all knew

I listened as we went around
the room to share our tale
amazed that everyone could
quickly come through without fail

Their images were clear and crisp:
a dog, a snake, a rabbit
It was as if they knew at once
or maybe it was habit

To think about themselves this way
took gathering some clues
How could they know their pieces fit
with cats or kangaroos?

That sinking feeling reappeared
the one where I'm divergent
Am I lion or a frog?
I couldn't choose.  What torment!

I started feeling hot and faint
My turn was three away
I'm animated like a squirrel
I'll say that!  Save the day!

But though a squirrel can keep that pace
all day and through the night
I'm not unwavering at all
so squirrel can't be quite right

Sometimes I need to pull inside
more turtle-like in pace
collect myself and gather strength
to keep up with the race

I'm ready now to speak out loud
to overcome this hurdle
At last I've come to understand
I'll tell them I'm a **Squirrtle!**

## An Open Plea

Please don't doubt
what I conceal
I pay a price
The scars are real

Attempts to hide
what you will peel
just wear me out
I need to heal

Please don't say
it can't be so
because you've seen
me overflow

with energy
you thought, *Hey, whoa
She's faking this
It can't be so*

Please don't doubt
the things I feel
I've learned to cope
with this ordeal

I've reached a place
where I reveal
Don't close me down
or I'll reseal

# Backstage

Out there we mask
explain, defend
and surge

Backstage we smile
and really know

Out there we spin
stop cold, fail
yet shine

Backstage our eyes
knit tight a bond

Out there actors
amaze the crowds
with unique charms

Backstage we're raw yet
sheltered from attack

Out there we dwell
within a
spinning top

Backstage we share
a quest for calm

Out there our journey
brought us to
this place behind

Backstage we rally
before the next spectacle

## Black Hole

Where do the keys go
that rested on this table
the bottle of ketchup
phone numbers on a wrinkled paper
directions to the meeting
mail to be read, later?

Where is that idea
that sparked our yesterday
the book title
a neighbor's name
details from a great movie
how many scoops of coffee?

Where do things go
that hide to make us humble?
How can a concept excite us so
and then dissolve?
What crater confiscates unused notions
unreachable vagueness locked within?

## Block It Out

The clutter I see is the chaos I feel It stops me
from reaching goals from clearing out the mess
within and atop each desk at which I sit Will it ever
end this attack upon my comfort zone Will the time
ever come that I will be without a pile of overdue
things for more than an hour Even when clutter
is missing I find myself anxious for its return It is
a monster waiting to demean my every attempt I
long for a place that is simple and clear of bro-
chures cards notices articles that should be read
bills that need follow-up magazines to digest and
stuff that doesn't fall into any category

# But...It's Tuesday

My planner says
today I play
catch up

To-do's
comprise
a lengthy list

Savoring time
protected from
other demands

I rise with bounce
at the very thought
of checking off

My back
*vibrates* with
an energy that

won't settle down
that *wriggles*
*wildly*,  leaving

me unable to *sit*
Despite my planner
it seems I often work

*bestwithonlyseconds*
*wedgedbetween*
*notime*

## Chaos

They say I'm impulsive
I rush to say "wait!"
I dash to get things done
I sprint at the gate

I hurry to speak
before you are through
I fear that I'll lose
that thought, or a few

I dart on an errand
that's not life or death
but if I don't do it
I won't take a breath

Until I have finished
that thought rules my mind
There's chaos inside me
That renders me blind

# Coaching

The feather blows
up over and gone
picking up speed
with wind, the master
at all times

Soft and slight
sending image of
frail to the
ground below
that misreads

Quick, yet
never certain of
its destiny
often caught
in a branch or pond

Dismayed ground
puzzled
with doubt
by frivolous attempts
at fate

The action of
fluff aiming
to land
within the grasp
of hope

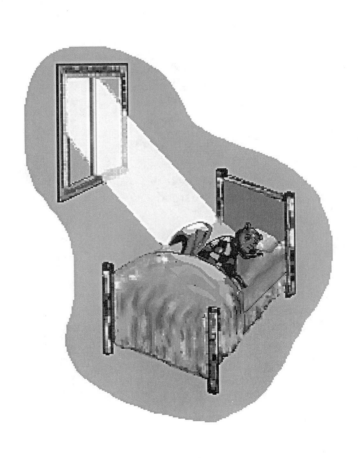

## Complete Bed Rest

six a.m.
still
quiet surroundings
rhythmic sounds

plan the day
the week, the month, the year
set the goals
higher still

energy surges
new ideas noted
flow from one
to still another

fire spreads
thoughts burst
ardor of silence
amazes the soul

unmoving never calm
breathing rapid
still struggling to hold
concepts in order

leaking
now spilling into
nowhere again
still

# Dancing On The Fringe

I stood dancing on the fringe
wildly waving
    many
    stopped
    to watch

I stood dancing on the fringe
loudly loving
    those who noticed
    whispered
    merit

I stood dancing on the fringe
wildly waving, loudly loving
    never keeping
    to the
    dance

Wildly waving
loudly loving
    much to do
    maybe later
    maybe never

Stranded
dancing
    on
    the
    fringe

## Detached

Staring
at the slowly moving branch
brittle blood red leaves break off
and drift to the ground
forming a variable pile

appearing
to enjoy departure
from life's demands, to admire the
yearly disunion of
child from parent

she sees
neither the tree
nor
the tender
division

Instead, a tense moment
is replayed
when the perfect
rebuttal was not
at hand

Waking, she
wonders how long
she has been gone
mind flips to a list of must-do's
cut in half, then half again

detached

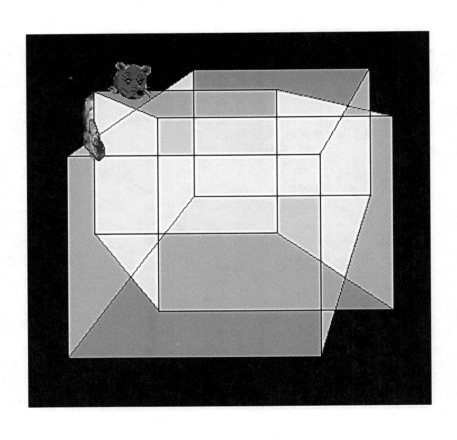

## Disparity

Crisis, I'm good at
I know what to do
I think very clearly
and will follow through

I carry out projects
that others won't touch
I wow 'em and please 'em
It doesn't take much

But while I am sharing
my plusses with you
I have to admit
there's another side too

The day to day things
that are easy for most
I can't seem to handle
like learning to coast

Crises, I'm good at
and this is no lie
it's life I can't master
I'm just not sure why

**Dread**


Shrouded
deep
within
erroneous clues
appearing
able
and alert
shamed
from the core
by discoveries
and near failures
she covers
and mourns
with
vigilance

## Embraceable You

Let's celebrate our differences
our glitches and our trials

Let's honor reckless moments
when we fumble up the aisles

Let's dedicate our focus
to all our special gifts

Let's praise the many talents
that hide amidst the rifts

Let's give up feeling hopeless
bemoaning all that fails

Let's concentrate our efforts
accepting when life pales

Let's sing about distinction
put pity up on shelves

Let's listen to Walt Whitman
and celebrate ourselves

**Focus**

silently
    staring
        I  believe
            I  know
                  you
              more
       than
   I  do
me

## Forgive Me

Forgive me, my loved ones
I've let you all down
when you least expect it
I've noticed the frown

Forgive me, my loved ones
It's noisy inside
my head as I struggle
I've honestly tried

Forgive me, my loved ones
for calls never made
for months that fly by
I appear to evade

Forgive me, my loved ones
I'm racing my car
on a track that keeps changing
I'm not getting far

Forgive me, my loved ones
I don't mean to shout
I'm stuck in a maze
and I often wear out

Forgive me, my loved ones
My feelings have cost
Please try to accept me
I often feel lost

# Help

Horace, hoping for harmony
hastily hammered
the hazardous hedge
holding the harem
of headstrong hares
from hightailing
the homestead

Elmer The Elder, eyeing this
episode, edged
effortlessly endowing
those engaged in endless
endeavors with everlasting
effectiveness

Losing the linkage, Lazy Leona lounged
Leery Lloyd lagged
and Lethargic Lonnie left
limiting the lonesome with
loss of luck

Plenty of preachers
provided the plans for
preventing this predicament
preferring to pressure
those present with perfect
prescriptions

Please

# I'm Destined For Greatness!

I'm destined for greatness
just around the corner

But, first I really need to
straighten up my desk

and re-do all my files
and get a new planner

and list all the steps to take
and research work-space

and locate those work-space catalogs
and where are those catalogs?

and here are my son's baby books...ohhhhhh
and I probably ought to toss out old catalogs

and touch up the scratches
and chips on the cabinet

I'm destined for
greatness!

Whew!

...and...

what was I saying?

### Illusion

Alone on a raft I drift
surrounded by
crystallized peaks of water
The moon smiles warmly
We have become
the dearest of friends

From the shore
crowds view
peace and
power, beauty and
perceived
serenity

But alone I drift
not wishing the peace
not understanding the power
not seeing the beauty
never reaping
the envied serenity

Staring upward
into nowhere
I rhythmically float
being led farther out
while still
the crowds observe

Let someone tell them
that on a raft
I cannot grow
or feel or laugh
or cry
I simply drift

### Let There Be

The wiring of my favorite lamp
seems frayed beyond repair
It happens that it sometimes works
so well that I would dare

to use it for a special night
when all must be *just so*
I'd hold my breath and say a prayer
the lamp would be aglow

and everyone would stop to say
that none has shined so well
that never has there been a lamp
as eager to excel

At other times I hate to say
the very same sweet light
would flicker at annoying times
I'd try with all my might

to figure out the pattern
the key to breaking down
Why sometimes we'd have noontime
just followed by sundown

And as I thought I *had it*
the lamp would cease to work
I'd try a million strategies like
giving it a jerk

But off it stayed by mystery
no matter what I'd do
My favorite lamp was giving up
Our fellowship was through

Just as I went to pack it up
feeling I'd been failed
that lamp again came through for me
you'd never know it ailed

Again it lit the room so bright
no other one could match
I'll never get it figured out
What makes it just...detach?

## Lima Beans, Broccoli And Liver

Dear God,

Me again.  In eleven years
I've never needed your help more than NOW
If you keep Mrs. Grass from calling on me
I *promise*...I'll even eat **lima beans!**

I try hard to remember what I read
but I keep thinking *she's about to call on me*
Please God, I don't want to be a pest
but I'm desperate!

My heart pounds so loud
that I'm sure Sarah will hear it
Sarah
always has the right answers

While you're at it God, could you please explain
why
Sarah
always has the right answers?

She doesn't seem much smarter than me
She hardly has any friends
She can't think of things to say at lunch
She's slower at her work

Mrs. Grass says we have 20 minutes
to read the chapter
Then we're having an out-loud test
I'm watching Sarah carefully

She's opened the book, looked at the clock
smiled and begun to read
Her eyes have moved across the page
and down to the bottom

I've opened my book, looked at the clock
smiled and begun to read
My eyes have moved across the page
and down to the bottom

Sarah's going on to the next page, breathing easily
never losing her smile
*I*...have absolutely no idea what I just read
I'm starting to pant

Time is up
The out-loud test is about to begin
Mrs. Grass is pleased with Sarah's answer
She's hunting for her next victim

I'll look down...she may forget I'm here
My heart is making such a racket
God
add...**broccoli** to those lima beans!

I've asked to take the book home
but I'm told that
*we can't make exceptions*
*It wouldn't be fair*

Not fair?   God, I have to be honest
with you here...excuse me if I sound rude
What's unfair is that *everyone* else
seems to know the answers but me

Everyone else must have gotten to you faster
*...Was there a form that I forgot to fill out*
*in order to get my wish?*

Mrs.   Grass   is   speaking   in   slow
motion   now   She's   calling   out
my   name   but   it   sounds   like
she's   under   water   I'm   standing

My knees are wiggling and my head is throbbing
I'm hot and can hardly breathe…Sarah bites her
nails real short, but the corners of her papers are
so neat and flat…mine are all curly and smudged

My mouth is open
The wall is coming down
GOD…add **LIVER** to the **BROCCOLI**
and **LIMA BEANS!** Final offer

Mrs. Grass' lipstick always looks bright
It goes straight across her mouth
She doesn't have those little peaks in her top lip
like other earthlings do

I'll tell her
I'm going to throw up
No…I'll tell her
I'm missing that chapter…

Mrs. Grass has the coldest eyes
They're eating right through me
I'm shrinking
Everything else is moving
so far away
She's got me, God
I promised her I'd try harder next time

I just wish
I knew how

## May I Rest In Peace

What if I'm jumpy in Heaven?
What if I'm still A.D.D?
What if I tried all my life to evolve
only to find ME is ME?

What if my wings need dry-cleaning?
What if I can't find my harp?
What if I'm asked to recall my good deeds
but find my thinking's not sharp?

What if my cloud is too messy?
What if I still shut right down?
What if I feel too embarrassed to try
to entertain angels in town?

What if I'm faking in Heaven?
Wouldn't that be the worst sin?
What if I can't rest in peace in that place?
What a thought! Eternal spin!

## Memory

Light closes
calms the sails
assaults the branches
disrobes women

The soul
the fool of small lies
of fire
souls of death
of sea
put out the struggle

He speaks of anger...no...courage
to go onward
He sees the light in night
The bell rings
out of fear

## Nomads

Most people love dinner parties
a chance to chat, sip wine
and engage in
sparkling conversation

For many of us
it's not that simple
We hear
a piece of this

while still being a part
of that
We are seduced from
across the

room by a word
or a name
that tugs
at our ear

and carries us
from where we
are to
somewhere else

We're always
on route
to that *other* place...

## Ode To A Pointing Finger


Oh sure, I could have accomplished anything
if I had just buckled down
if I had just paid attention
if I had just sat still
if I had just concentrated
if I had just applied myself
if I had just studied
if I had just cared more
if I had just valued the goal
if I had just disciplined myself
if I had just been more organized
if I had just not been in such a hurry
if I had just
not been
me

**Oh, Now I Get It**

Power is not asking
    yet others offer
    silence that brings dignity
    digesting turmoil
    the exquisite Fall
    uniquely noticed
    adventure, discomfort and growth
    replacing fear

Power is adaptation
    to eyesight and hearing
    perception
    opinion and dogma
    humor from stress
    reality from imagination
    sitting as
    standing becomes impossible

Power is hearing arias
    hearing optimism
    feeling a cat
    feeling content
    seeing colors
    seeing grays
    tasting hot fudge
    tasting success

Power is maturity
    amassing life
    priorities carefully shaped
    creating collage
    freedom to dare
    to fail
    comfortable skin
    translucent yet strong

## Organizationally Challenged

A monster
lurks around the phone
comes in with the mail
and nests shrewdly on the desk

The lascivious gargoyle
breeds quickly
producing
abundant offspring

Within seconds
the air is filled
with stuff-dust
choking

out all
hope for
clear
ideas

## Out To Lunch

Beyond the racing waiters
thin glasses clink
sweet melodies
intended for
announcement
of a special
toast
as smoke rings
float beyond
view
a violin purrs
never heard

# Reaching For Perfect

Would the grass
grow orange
if
we just let go?

Would they read
our name
on
the radio?

Would we shrink
a lot
or
have vertigo?

If they teach
us how
can
we let

it go?

## Show Time!

Collect them all upon the shelf
the clowns, each magic little elf
a face, a mask for all to see
Do not remove
it's only me

I paint a smile, I fix a laugh
the fool, the human photograph
To hide it all, the victory
Please don't remove
it's only me

The saddened eyes are not a clue
the downward smile, the worn tattoo
the tattered clothes
the bright red nose
I need to keep my heart from you

Collect them all upon the shelf
the clowns, so many sides of self
a face, a front, a farce, not free
Please don't remove
it's only me

## Swift Shift


Faultless sky
Thursday
dreamy possibilities
limitless plan

No warning
Friday leaps
dense obscurity
endless roadblocks

forgotten goals
lost in fog
blemished
fragments

Yesterday's passion
shifts
gnarled
cobwebs

familiar
unwelcome
barriers flaw
clarity

p i e c e s   s t r u g g l e
t o
r e
u
n
i
t
e

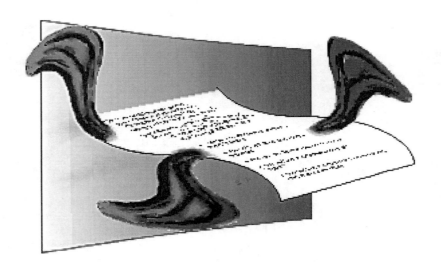

## Tails From The Silver Screen

What we need
in this life
is a script
a sequential path
to follow
where the plot
is known
before the
movie begins

We could listen
as the music
guides us
this way
or that
without
the questioning
torment
of fog

...did someone forget
to send me
my script?

## The Great Wall

Blocking the view
for 1,500 miles
a Wonder of the World
exists
to divide
ideas, people and clues

I too
possess a wall
within my head
that comes and goes
existing to divide
ideas, people and clues

I see no greatness
in my wall
only a struggle
to remove or
see around its
unforgiving presence

# The Other Me

Frenzied
    darting
        dashing
           dodging

Clever
    planning
        plotting
           pushing

Social
    mixing
        mending
           molding

**and** then

Time to pull in
regroup the tired soul
feel the peace
of aloneness
heal the hurts
and feel the power
of capability
Time to be
the other me

# The Princess And The "P"


Back in a time, in the land of Parnay
there lived a Fair Princess perfecting each day
She paled all her subjects Her prowess would pass
the high expectations of this public lass

The Princess appeared peaceful and in control
perched high as she handled her Kingdom, her role
With strong perseverance her energy peaked
allowing completion of all that she seeked

Partaking new projects this prim phantom found
she paid a huge price to personify "sound"
For buried beneath the prism of real
a paradox lurked just waiting to peel

back layered protection well hiding the pain
Discovery unveiled the panicked domain
the place where her talents were always in doubt
the paradox showing her *with* or *without*

## Unplugged

In a crowd
in that moment
when we fear
when it's quiet
our turn to speak
our introductions
a comment
an answer
we begin
we search
lost thought
lost answers
hearts pound
hearts broken
Unplugged

**Very Well Red**


Books call me to their megastores
where feeling slippery covers
settles my *jumpy juices*
I really love books

Carefully chosen page markers
peer up over the top
of clean, closed, creaseless
bodies of beautiful thought

I plan to retain
cohesive
memory exciting
my sense of understanding

At dinner groups
ideas are extracted
from shiny cases
critiqued and digested

*Am I reading*
*a good book?*
*Of course*
*Not quite finished*

*but, yes, so engrossing*
*Name ?  Author ?*
foggy....idea, incomplete
familiar curtain.... going down

I'm very well red

**Workplace Sorrows**


Cluttered desks
Fluorescent lights
Rooms that have no windows

Lack of color
Nothing soft
Noisy atmosphere woes

Sudden changes
Hot, still air
Voices rise to high lows

Magic disappearing notes
Papers hide
Where time goes.....

Remember when you were a kid
Well, part of us still is...
which leads us to work sorrows

# For Parents

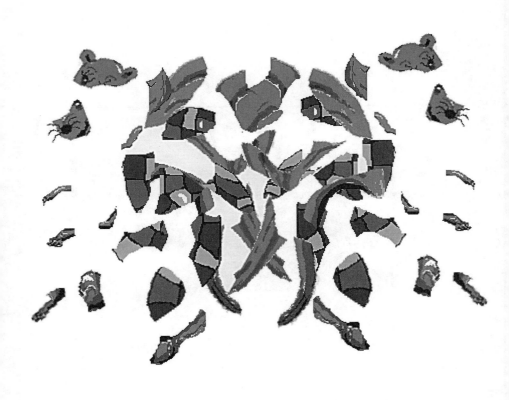

**5,4,3,2,1.......**


When your chaos
met mine
an explosion
occurred
that wiped
us both
out

When your energy
met mine
a creation
erupted
that
sent us
blissfully spinning

When your hurt
met
mine
fury
crept
into our
hearts and yet

When your love
met mine
we melted
into
soft
sad
understanding

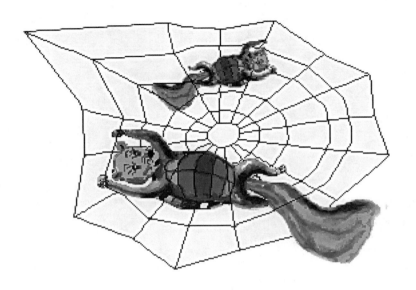

## Dear Rick

I can only imagine
what it was like
for you
in the elastic days

when each unit of time
brought sprinting surprise
creative and warm
or bewildered and frustrated

We spent our gifted existence
together, you and I
making our way
through a sticky web

often advancing happily
often stuck in confusion
reaching each other
from a primal place

I am grateful for your
endless love and patience
while I learned what
the web was all about

for your good-natured
smile, your warm arms
around my neck
You dear child

you thought I knew
what I was doing
that all parents were
elastic, sometimes strong

sometimes weak without
warning. You coped with
each stretch, though you
paid a price

Thank you, my first-born
for your trusting spirit
that allowed me to learn
the treasure of parenting

I love you

## Did You Take Your...?


Never mind.  I can tell
You see
I love you both
The you
that sits
exploring
an idea
The you
that takes
the time
to reflect
and dream
The you
that speaks
of goals
and s-t-e-p-s
along the way

and

The you
that does not
*fit*
into the
*maze*
The you
that opens
up his heart
to feel it all
at once
Admit them both, my love

# Fingers In A Long Bath

You're asleep
finally
I wonder with
all my heart
if I can do again tomorrow
what I did
today

There isn't a
part of me
that isn't
numb from
the battle we fought
today

Your will
locked with mine
every ticking minute
lost forever
today

We built
tense
photographs
today

I won
but, at what cost
today?

You gave up, undiminished
today

We both shriveled today

## For My Children

Parenting you
is the single
most challenging
task
attempted
Loving you
allows
purity
of pride
and pain

Guiding you
requires being
all that
I can
at all times
Disappointing you
breaks us
each apart
at our
center

Perhaps you
would be
without pain
had you
not been mine
Bless you
for the mirror
you hold up
reflecting
us both

## Love Me For What I am

I'm not the patient, quiet kind
collecting facts, deciding odds
I can't sit back and be the lamb
Please love me for what I am

Protect I will, share all I know
make you aware of what I've learned
I'm not a fake.  I give a damn
Please love me for what I am

    I can't live in your fantasy
    I'm only what you see right now
    I've grown a lot to where I am
    I want the chance to show you how

I'll teach you how to taste life's fruit
to be so proud of who you are
to feel inside...your own program
Please love me for what I am

## Make A Wish Come True

If we see a bird
struggling to fly
can we keep it safe
can we help it try?

Can a robin be
just for one brief time
all that it can be
an eagle in its mind?

Brighten one small life
Make a wish come true
Magic's all around
It depends on you

If we see a flower
threatened by a storm
can we keep it strong
can we keep it warm?

Can a dreamer be
if only for a day
smiling in the sun
blessed and on his way?

## Sir Allofus D. Dashalot

Once upon a
silly time
there lived
Sir Allofus

who tried each
day to overcome
the missing of
his bus

He tried to
get up earlier
to brush and
floss and run

to eat a
balanced breakfast
and get his
planning done

But though his
mind would wander
his files were all
marked "Hot"

He never
gave up
trying...
Sir **A. D. D**ashalot

## Stepping Back


Last week I urged a young mother
to relax and let her miracle unfold
Her thoughts were
endless wanderings into the future
darting at all the "maybes" and
"nevers" until she was certain
of all probable dangers

Last week I urged a young mother
to relax and let her miracle unfold
After a cup of lukewarm tea
she admitted feeling so much better
and just knew she would never
fall apart again; I assured her that
she would, but all would be fine

Last week I urged a young mother
to relax and let her miracle unfold
as I struggled to block out
the memories of a well-guarded secret
all parents must agree
to store deep down
where slip-ups can be hushed

Last week I urged a young mother
to relax and let her miracle unfold
despite the scene that her child
displayed at the mall
Last week I cried to an old woman
at my table as she urged me
to relax and let my miracle unfold

**Storms**


There's a sadness in me
as I watch you grow
taking in the multitude of firsts
   some strengthen your core
   others threaten to destroy


There's a sadness in me
as I think of the risks
words that puncture
   being ignored
   acceptance of never-to-be dreams


There's a sadness in me
as I watch you grow
I cannot provide shelter
   Please dress warm
   Storms do damage

## Ten Worst Parenting Moments

1. You're the nursery school parent singing
   *Wheels on the Bus*, while *your* child destroys clay
   creations

2. You're the kindergarten parent at *Open
   House*, praying as you scan the displayed drawings

3. You're the sports-observing parent holding
   your breath at another *swing and a miss*

4. You're the confused parent struggling to remember
   the latest *bargaining contract*

5. You're the middle-school parent being told
   you have18 minutes to produce home-baked treats

6. You're the breathless parent dropping off the mis-
   placed termpaper on due date afternoon

7. You're the mathematical parent calculating
   the remaining painful parent-teacher conferences

8. You're the teen's parent in daily battle where
   gasoline meets candles

9. You're the high school parent weary from the
   voyage

10. You're the enlightened parent learning that
    the exhausting contest is forever

## Will He Make A Mom Of Me?

I was bored
and he was cranky
I felt guilty
He felt wet
I relaxed some
He worked puzzles
I was proud
My little pet

I was anxious
Duties piled
He was tired
Couldn't sleep
Stomach's knotted
Stomach's gassy
Work's accomplished
Not a peep

*Took a short nap?*
*Glad to see you*
Guess he reads between clenched teeth
He's unhappy
God I'm trying
Have a cookie
Try a Heath

He's in bed now
I'm exhausted
Think I'll change
my strategy
I'll unwind more
He'll unwind more
Will he make a Mom of me?

115

# Introducing Charlotte Booth

## About Charlotte Booth:

Charlotte-Louise Brewster Booth was born on May 9, 1983. She currently enjoys Latin and Science, due to teachers that are especially "fun and enthusiastic." She enjoys spending time with her friends, traveling, camping, biking, soccer and field hockey.

Charlotte lives in Michigan, with her mom, Becky, dad, John, big brother, Johnny, and a "few" pets – 3 dogs: Shadow, Peter and Splash; 3 birds: Bubbles, Blaze and Montego; and 18 ferrets: Soozie, Ursah, Archie, Flora, Emilie, Angus, Thud, Ping, Lola, Fiona, Hummer, Al, Pogo, Spats, Bungee, Suess, Loki and Iggy.

Now an Honor Roll student, Charlotte was diagnosed with ADD while in the fifth grade. At the time that she wrote the following poem, *Trapped*, Charlotte was twelve years old and in the seventh grade. She speaks from the heart as she shares her tender feelings related to entering her teens with this disorder. Yet, she states that "I've always had it [ADD] and have been this way. This is normal."

A bright, creative young lady, Charlotte demonstrates a strong sense of honesty and sensitivity within her expressive sharings. The joy she experiences in writing reminds me so much of *The Me* at her age. I think she is a good example of what understanding and acceptance of ADD can do to allow a youngster to "go with her strengths." It is a pleasure to introduce her at this time.

**Trapped**
by Charlotte Booth


I feel trapped
like I'm in a cage
screaming
screaming
trapped
trapped

My heart is confused
I am changing
people changing
life changing
all new things

coming
coming at
me

I feel safe
in the cage
but
trapped
while
safe

Life is different
I am different
HELP!

# Suggested References

The following list is not meant to be inclusive, but is a starting point for gaining information on ADD.

Barkley, R.A. (1990). *Attention Deficit Hyperactivity Disorder: A Handbook for Diagnosis and Treatment*. New York: Gilford Press.

Bramer, J.S. (1996). *Succeeding in College with Attention Deficit Disorders: Issues and Strategies for Students, Counselors, and Educators*. Plantation, FL: Specialty Press.

Bramer, J.S. & Fellman, W.R. (1997). *Success in College and Career for Adults with Attention Deficit Disorders* (Video). Plantation, FL: Specialty Press.

Goldstein, S. (1996). *Managing Attention Disorders and Learning Disability in Late Adolescence and Adulthood*. New York: Wiley Interscience Press.

Hollowell, E.M. & Ratey, J.J. (1994). *Driven to Distraction*. New York: Pantheon Books.

Hollowell, E.M. & Ratey, J.J. (1994). *Answers to Distraction*. New York: Pantheon Books.

Hartman, T. (1993). *Attention Deficit Disorder: A Different Perception*. New York: Pantheon Press.

Kelly, K. & Ramundo, P. (1993). *You Mean I'm Not Lazy, Stupid or Crazy?!* Cincinnati, OH: Tyrell & Jerem Press.

Latham, P.S. & Latham, P.H. (Eds.) (1994). *Succeeding in the Workplace*. Washington, DC: JKL Communications.

Nadeau, K.G. (1996). *Adventures in Fast Forward: Life, Love, and Work for the ADD Adult*. New York: Brunner/Mazel, Inc.

Solden, S. (1995). *Women with Attention Deficit Disorder*. Grass Valley, CA: Underwood Books.

Weiss, G., & Hechtman, L. (1993). *Hyperactive Children Grown Up* (2nd ed.). New York: Guilford Press.

Weiss, L. (1992). *Attention Deficit Disorder in Adults*. Dallas, TX: Taylor Publishing Company.

Weiss, L. (1992). *ADD on the Job: Making your ADD Work for You*. Dallas, TX: Taylor Publishing Company.

Wender, P.H. (1987). *The Hyperactive Child, Adolescent, and Adult*. New York: Oxford University Press.